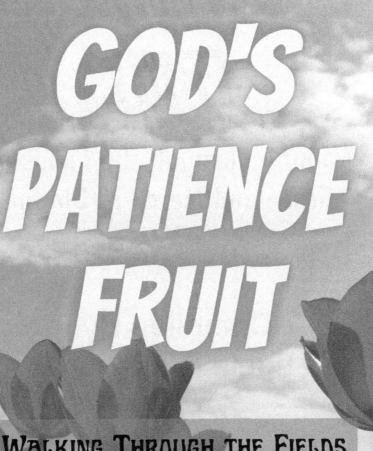

Angela R. Edwards

GOD'S PATIENCE FRUIT

Walking Through the Fields of Grace and Mercy in Bloom

Compiled By:
Angela R. Edwards

Redemption's Story Publishing, LLC, Harlem, GA (USA)

God's Patience Fruit:
Walking Through the Fields of Grace and Mercy in Bloom

Copyright © 2022
Angela R. Edwards

All Rights Reserved.
In accordance with the U.S. Copyright Act of 1976, the scanning, uploading, and electronic sharing of any part of this book without the author's or publisher's permission is unlawful piracy and theft of the author's intellectual property. If you would like to use material from this book (other than brief quotations for literary reviews), we ask you to please cite your reference.
Thank you for your support of the author's rights.

Scripture references are used with permission from Zondervan via Biblegateway.com. Public Domain.
Unless otherwise stated with the contributor's name, quotes used are from The Goal Chaser via TheGoalChaser.com.

Print ISBN 13: 978-1-948853-57-6
Digital ISBN 13: 978-1-948853-58-3
Library of Congress Control Number: 2022946590

Redemption's Story Publishing, LLC
Angela Edwards, CEO
P.O. Box 639
Harlem, GA 30814
RedeemedByHim@Redemptions-Story.com

Dedication

This book is dedicated to
EVERY SINGLE PERSON
who reads it.

Why ***EVERYONE***?

The answer is simple:
We **ALL** have times when we lose our
PATIENCE—
for one reason or another.

May this piece of literary art bring
PEACE
to your impatient moments.

Acknowledgments

First and foremost, I give all glory, honor, and praise to the **Holy Trinity**: God the Father, God the Son, and God the Holy Spirit. I am nothing without Him and remain ever grateful and humbled for the gifts He instilled in me. My life has not been the same since I accepted Him as my Personal Lord and Savior.

I cannot fail to mention my PATIENT husband, **James Edwards**. Many days and many nights, he sacrificed "our" time so that I could continue my tireless work of helping others share their God-inspired messages. I love you!

To my mother and BIGGEST cheerleader on this side of Heaven, **Marlowe R. Scott**: I appreciate your **PATIENT** hand with me from the days of my youth until this very day. When my life was going all willy-nilly, you allowed me to make my mistakes but were always there, praying and waiting for me to "get it right." For that, for your contributions to this project, for being my "second eye," and for SO much more, I thank you. I love you!

To **Dr. Marilyn E. Porter**, my bestie for as long as I can remember: Our days date to The Little Red Schoolhouse in our little hometown, but we know God had pre-ordained that first meeting for such a time as this in adulthood. Thank you for writing this Foreword and MANY others, for being my friend to the end, and for supporting me on every venture and adventure I take. I love you!

To the host of Contributing Authors of God's Patience Fruit (in no particular order); **Tosha R. Dearbone, Marlowe R. Scott, Desirae Jefferson, Reyna Harris-Goynes, Rev. George Swift, Laurie Benoit, and Evangelist Keywana Wright-Jones**: You were the ones who "remained," fulfilled your commitment, and pushed your way through to completion. From the side stories shared with me, I am aware that this project tested you…and your **PATIENCE**. The enemy came for you, **BUT GOD!** I am grateful for the words of wisdom and love each of you shared within your stories and look forward to seeing what God will do with your evangelical works. You are my sisters- and brother-in-Christ here on earth and beyond. I love you **ALL** and truly appreciate each of you living this Fruit of the Spirit with me. God Bless!

Last, but far from least, to my immediate and extended family and social media following: I see you! When you may think I'm not noticing or appreciative of your every click or comment, please know that **I AM**. Together, our words effect change in the atmosphere. Don't stop being whom God says you are! Blessings to you today and every day!

Foreword
By Rev. Dr. Marilyn E. Porter

To walk in a life of patience is indeed a triumph! More often than not, patience is a reward for having endured the extreme outcomes of impatience. I have often said, "For every action, there is an opposite and equal reaction." (Well, I am sure someone else—perhaps Isaac Newton—said it first, but I believe in the principle strongly.) So, it would seem that the opposite of patience is impatience.

Not so!

The opposite of patience is…are you ready? **PRIDE!** Yes, **PRIDE!** To be impatient is feeling as if one is too important to be made to wait—the belief that one's needs are greater than the process.

I recall living in the Washington, DC area about 22 years ago. I had a job that was accurately 1.2 miles from my home, yet it would sometimes take me 45 minutes or an hour to get home from work during rush-hour traffic. I would be livid every day when I finally walked through the door—angry and frustrated because it should not have taken so long. Clearly, every person on the highway experienced the same exact process, but in my mind—my **prideful** mind—I was the only one affected by the slow-moving traffic.

One day, the Holy Spirit arrested me. Instead of being grateful that I was going home to my children...instead of being thankful for the job that helped my family go on vacations and allowed my then-husband and me to send money to our mothers...instead of taking that time to listen to a sermon or worship, I was mad at the process of getting home. I suffered from a nasty case of impatience, and right now—even today—I must pray my way through traffic. The difference is that I pray for everyone on the road, not just myself.

Patience is a Fruit of the Spirit that regulates our spirit man. I would dare to say that much of what we label "anxiety" is simply a bad case of impatience. When we push against the process—the timing of God—we lose our joy and peace. In turn, our physical bodies respond in various negative ways, including:

- High blood pressure
- Migraine headaches
- Muscles tighten
- Cardiovascular (breathing) problems
- Digestive issues
- Weakened immune system

Various other physical and mental issues can be traced to one's inability to sit in patience and allow God to navigate the moments. Trust that **HE KNOWS** the exact timing of each and every single one of our "unique" experiences.

"But let patience have her perfect work, that ye may be perfect and entire, wanting nothing" (James 1:4).

I have often pondered: What is "her perfect work." It is only now, as I sit to pen these words, that I realize fully:

PATIENCE WORKS PEACE.

So, I leave you with a charge: Take note of those moments that require patience and work diligently to sustain the peace that patience brings.

Lastly, remember always: God knows and orchestrates each moment of your life perfectly and in His own time.

Rev. Dr. Marilyn E. Porter
Founder, PPIC
www.marilyneporter.com

"Trust the process. Your time is coming. Just do the work and the results will handle themselves."

~ Tony Gaskins ~

Core Scripture

"But the fruit of the Spirit [the result of His presence within us] is love [unselfish concern for others], joy, [inner] peace, patience [not the ability to wait, but how we act while waiting], kindness, goodness, faithfulness, gentleness, self-control. Against such things, there is no law."

Galatians 5: 22-23, Amplified Bible

Introduction

Patience. *What is it? Why is it even a Fruit of the Spirit?* Perhaps the synonyms "longsuffering," "endurance," or "perseverance" are more relatable. Let's examine a simple yet thorough definition from a biblical perspective.

"Patience is the quality of restraint that prevents believers from speaking or acting hastily in the face of disagreement, opposition, or persecution" (Rose Publishing, 2008).

From that definition alone, we can see why acquiring the skill of being patient is critical. Being patient is a Fruit of the Spirit, so I believe it is not something that can be taught; we must practice...and practice...and practice daily. When walking in the Spirit, you cannot say, *"I don't feel like doing it today."* No. A Christian virtue does not disappear when opposition and obstacles come your way. As such, God's Patience Fruit is the thing that makes this virtue a Christian one—whether or not you're a believer. What may be even more comforting is knowing our forgiving Heavenly Father knows that in our humanness, we will not always walk in His Fruits 100% of the time—but we should strive for it, ask for forgiveness when we knowingly (and unknowingly) do not, and repent for our wrongdoings.

Moving forward, when you find yourself anxious, unhappy, restless, or impatient, work towards a healthier outlook on life. Seek stability and learn to practice patience in every situation you encounter that tests your resolve to, well, **BE PATIENT!** Make patience so typical in your life that you gain stability when faced with things that try to demand that you step out of character—God's character. *#WWJD* (What Would Jesus Do?)

Yes, walking in the Spirit takes practice. Haven't you heard, *"Practice makes perfect"*?

Yes, you will have an occasional misstep, but do not lose heart. Get back on the path and K.I.M. (Keep It Moving)!

Yes, there will be times when you completely **LOSE IT** (as you will read in the stories contained herein) but realize there's a level of normalcy to the moment...for just a moment. Don't stay in that place of negativity. It's unhealthy! Take the time to just breathe. You will be alright and ready to take on whatever adversity the enemy throws at you next—because he will come for you. Please don't let that stop you from always being prepared. Use the spirit of discernment that is in you to recognize his antics.

Today, please take the time to applaud your **PATIENCE** level up to this point in your life. No matter where you are in your walk with Christ, He sees and knows all. He knows your heart. He knows your why. He knows **YOU**. Be encouraged! God is not through with you yet! *Amen and Amen!*

Table of Contents

Dedication vi

Acknowledgments vii

Foreword ix

   By Rev. Dr. Marilyn E. Porter

Core Scripture xiii

Introduction xiv

Patience Word Cloud xix

What is Patience? 1

   By Rev. George Swift

Patience: Tolerating Delays and Sufferings 11

   By Marlowe R. Scott

Patience: A Poem 21

   By Marlowe R. Scott

The Pressure of "The Wait" 23

   By Angela R. Edwards

Patience: A Universal Lesson 32

   By Laurie Benoit

God Has Me on Hold 42

   By Tosha Dearbone

Fighting My Way to Patience 53

   By Desirae Jefferson

Patience Set Me Free from the Past 59

   By Reyna Harris-Goynes

Waiting in Silence 64

   By Evangelist Keywana Wright-Jones

Conclusion 70

It's Time to Reflect on Your Patience Level 72

About the Compiler 85

Other Books in the Series 89

God's Patience Fruit

Patience Word Cloud

Angela R. Edwards

God's Patience Fruit

What is Patience?
By Rev. George Swift

Webster's College Dictionary and Thesaurus® defines patience as *"The quality of being able to calmly wait or endure."* That sounds good and might work for some who think they can control any situation that comes their way, but what happens when it is beyond their control? I used to think like that. If "it" did not go how I wanted it to, I would just bail out. That way of thinking caused me a lot of pain and suffering in my life, but I was too stubborn to change—even though I knew there was a good reason for me to make that change!

In the past, I never had any real guidance or structure on how to think or analyze a situation, so I often acted on impulse. If it felt right, I did it. If it didn't, I dismissed it. It is easy to have patience regarding things that are pleasurable and make you feel good, but when it goes the other way, that creates a problem with control over your patience. I used to think that I was a very patient person. The truth of the matter was that I had no patience at all. I was always angry and did not trust anyone...which was not a good match for patience because being patient means being kind, understanding, caring, and loving.

I was none of those things.

Today, I define patience as ***"Trusting in GOD and waiting on Him to answer."*** Let's see what the scriptures say.

"Be anxious for nothing, but in everything by prayer and supplication, with thanksgiving, let your requests be known to God; and the peace of God, which surpasses all understanding, will guard your hearts and minds through Christ Jesus" (Philippians 4:6-8, NKJV).

One of the things I feared the most was going on dialysis—so much so that I put in my Living Will that if anything would happen to me and I had to go on dialysis, do not hook me up because I would rather die. That same sentiment was shared with my daughter.

Well...

In 2017, after getting into a serious motorcycle accident, I prayed to God to give me the patience to get through that ordeal. I told Him I would try to look at things in a more spiritual light instead of my human eyes. *(Be careful what you ask of God because He will test you to see if you are serious.)*

For some people, patience is tested while waiting at a stop light or waiting on the results of a test. For others, patience might be holding out for a better job or waiting for the perfect person to come along *(there is no "perfect person" walking this earth)*. Still, for others, patience means waiting for a newborn baby to arrive, hoping that child is "normal." For me, patience goes a little deeper than any of those things.

In the Old Testament Book of Job, we read that he had to endure many hardships in order to understand what 'patience' truly meant. I, too, had to be tried and tested to understand what I was asking of God. We all go through seasons when our patience is tested, and our lives feel like we are in an outright battle on all sides. Relationships aren't working. Situations at work are tenuous. We receive a bad health report. The list is endless!

What to do in those difficult situations and many others like them? How do we stay confident and hopeful when life feels like a struggle? Where can we go for strength and safety? The answer to those questions is this: In seasons when life feels like a battle, win the war by worshipping God and always maintain your faith.

For me, I do not separate the good times or the hard times from my faith. Today, I am blessed to have my life covered with the gift of faith. I have taken an oath to have my relationship with Jesus (God) be as authentic a relationship as I would have with a physical, real person. I ask Jesus for His wisdom to look at situations I am in with His eyes and be able to walk with His heart. And finally, I lay all my struggles before God. His wisdom and love give me confidence and hope, even when my human emotions struggle.

Patience is demonstrated in several different stages depending on what is happening to an individual at any given time. There is no absolute certainty on how you are going to handle a situation until you are confronted with the dilemma.

To say I know how I will react in any given situation is like saying I am going to live forever—and we all know that is not true.

In July 2020, I learned what true patience, trust, and belief in God really meant. I had to have brain surgery, and my daughter was told I had to go on dialysis, or I would die that night after surgery. That was a very hard decision for her to make because it meant going against my wishes and Living Will. I had no patience for dialysis and told her I would rather die than be put on a machine for four hours, three times a week, with two large needles in my arm that withdrew blood from my body and then returned it to my system, leaving me very weak and fatigued. Mentally, I was not prepared for that process, nor did I think I could physically endure such an ordeal but (as you will read), I agreed to go. It took every ounce of patience I had for me to continue going to dialysis after leaving my 40-day rehab center stay. As a matter of fact, I had decided that once I got home, I would discontinue going to dialysis.

In order for me to accept the fact that I had to either go to dialysis or die, I turned it into a game and called it "Work." Just like with any job, you must put in the time to receive a paycheck and (hopefully) get rewarded, promoted, and, maybe one day, retire. I started going to "Work" three days a week for four hours each day. That continued for about six months when my "Boss" (Dr. Shergill) noticed my performance was improving, so he adjusted my hours to three-and-a-half hours, three times a week. As time went on, I continued to improve, so my hours were changed once again to three hours, three times a week. I had to put in a lot of hard work to achieve that goal. It took a lot of patience to get up each day and go to "Work," when all I wanted to do was just give up—but I kept hearing a voice that reminded me how far **GOD** had brought me, so I kept pressing on toward the mark. That same voice would constantly tell me to stop grumbling, arguing, and complaining and be thankful for what I have so that I may be blameless and pure before God for what He had already done for me *(and is still doing)*.

On what basis should a child of God not complain? What makes us different than the rest of the world? Well, we should know that our Heavenly Father is in control of all things. We know that some of the inconveniences we experience may actually be divine opportunities to help someone else or be used for God to grow us. Either way, complaining does not honor God. Besides, complaining never makes things better.

Through that whole process, I learned that if I had the faith—even as small as a mustard seed—I could say to my mountain, "Move from here to there," and it will move. Nothing would be impossible. (See Matthew 17:20.)

Determined to get off dialysis, I had to change my attitude about my condition and lifestyle. I did not know how long it would take, but I knew I would not let dialysis control my life. I was going to be in control of how I accepted my condition. For 21 months, I faithfully went to "Work" until one day, my "Boss" came into the center and stated to me that I had reached the level where I no longer had to "Work" because I was dialysis-free! What a **HALLELUJAH** moment that was—not only for me but for everyone else! If you believe God can do it and put in the work, it can also happen for you!

No matter what your problem may be or what your addiction is, it is not too big for God to fix it. All you have to do is surrender to Him and believe in Him with your whole heart, soul, and mind. Claim the victory, and it will be done. I'm a living witness and living miracle that if you develop a loving, intimate relationship with Jesus, He will grant your heart's desire.

Now, understand this: Patience does not come automatically. I believe having patience means not allowing people or problems to push your buttons or get on your last nerve to the point that you act irrationally and lose control *(that's when the devil has victory over you, and that dishonors God's intentions for your life)*. You must pray often and trust God wholly, no matter the situation confronting you. By doing so, you will find that you can handle the problem in a calm, rational manner.

The following scripture passages may help you along the way and provide further clarity on your personal walk with Christ. **Psalm 1:1-6** sums up how we should live our lives and sets the pattern for how we can continue to be patient in today's trying times. Though we are not promised an easy life, we are told that Christ will be there with us when we believe in Him and that He will never give us more than we can handle with His help. In **2 Corinthians 12:9**, we read how even in our hard times, they can be used to glorify God.

When I reflect on what it takes to be patient and have patience, I only have to look at the life of Jesus. He was sent into the world by His Father to save us from a life of sin and damnation. During His 33 years on earth, He endured all kinds of humiliation, suffering, and abuse while doing the work He was sent to do. Through it all, He never complained or gave up on the assignment that was given to Him. At the end of His life on earth, He stood firm on patience as He hung on the cross and asked His Father to "forgive them, for they know not what they are doing."

If only we show half as much patience, love, and kindness to our brothers and sisters as Jesus gave to us, this world would be a much better place. Imagine a world where we all respect and get along with one another...

Are you willing and bold enough to take that first step and truly live the life of Jesus? Or do you just want to continue going through this life just being human? The choice is yours. As for me, I'm trying to live out the rest of my life being the image God created me to be.

Finally, in order to have patience, one must take a rest from their laboring. Even God rested after He finished His creation. If our Creator rested, how much more do we—as His creation—need to rest? Taking time to rest teaches us to trust God because He never asks us to meet life's pressures and demands on our own power or by relying on our own strength. God invites us to enter His rest! Have you neglected your rest lately?

> *"Come to Me, all who labor and are heavy laden,*
> *and I will give you rest."*
> (Matthew 11:28, NKJV)

Angela R. Edwards

"Wait patiently on the Lord, and He will answer."

Rev. George Swift

Patience: Tolerating Delays and Sufferings

By Marlowe R. Scott

INTRODUCTION

As I share my experiences with you, prayerfully, they will help you learn why Patience is an essential attribute of the Fruit of the Spirit.

In my life experiences, "Patience" and "Tolerance" are words with similar meanings. Being told to "count to ten" when patience is needed or remembering the saying, "It is better to forgive and forget," didn't always work.

As I wrote my story, there were times when I found it challenging because I kept receiving poetic messages in my thoughts. Just to share, the following is the beginning of one such poetic experience:

"Patience is a virtue,

As we hear some people say.

The virtue to be achieved

Is not readily given to us

Along life's busy days."

Merriam-Webster® defines patience as "the capacity to accept or tolerate delay, trouble, or suffering without getting angry or upset." **WOW!** Is that a reality we can actually achieve? The answer is probably different for each of us.

Surprisingly, I also discovered that Patience is a girl's name of English origin. It means "enduring or forbearing" and has been a virtue-designated name since the 16th century. I found that fun fact interesting. Perhaps it was felt a male might not have been appropriate for the name because of their temperament.

A few scriptures offer examples of patience and its value, and I'll share a few here.

"And not so, but we glory in tribulations also: knowing that tribulations worketh patience; and patience, experience; and experience, hope." (Romans 5:3-4, KJV)

"But the Fruit of the Spirit is love, joy, peace, longsuffering, gentleness, goodness, faith, meekness, temperance; against such, there is no law." (Galatians 5:22-23)

"Better is the end of a thing than the beginning thereof: and the patient in spirit is better than the proud in spirit." (Ecclesiastes 7:8)

A GLIMPSE OF MY PERSONAL "PATIENCE" EXPERIENCES

Basically, I am a quiet, patient woman from a Christian home and small family. My parents were patient and tolerant as they raised me in New Jersey's farming area. Additionally, I had a mentally-challenged brother two years older than me whom I played with and helped teach him some childlike things such as games and songs as we grew up.

My most challenging experiences with patience were perhaps in my teen years. Going from a familiar small country school setting to a city high school, I was shy and overweight at the time. I let many remarks about my size pass me by without comment. Those words hurt, but I "sucked it up" (so to say). My intelligence, coupled with my family's love, was a plus on my side. By the time I graduated, I had gone from over 200 pounds to 140 pounds. All it took were months of eating less, exercising, and sticking to my goal.

PATIENCE AND TIME RESULTED IN A HEALTHY REWARD!

There were times when, as hard as it was, I didn't say what I was thinking when I was insulted, someone lied to me (or about me), hurt a family member, and more. I learned to smile, look them in the eye, and say, "God Bless you." Other times, I said nothing at all. My response—or lack thereof—resulted in them either leaving me alone or deciding to turn away when they saw me coming.

FACT: WORDS CAN HURT AND CANNOT BE TAKEN BACK ONCE SPOKEN.

Patience has been a fault of mine over the years. A prime example is that it took time for me to learn the lesson of trying to work with procrastinators! They have included family members, friends, and coworkers. Because I can usually accomplish a task in a reasonable time, I had (in the past) quit asking the individual(s) involved to do what they were asked to do and actually just went on and did it myself! **THAT WAS A MISTAKE, FOR SURE!** As a result, the procrastinators didn't change, leaving me to feel overworked and overcommitted to what they were responsible for. **THOSE DAYS ARE OVER!** Today, I remind them and, after the second or third time, just let the work go undone.

Before going further with scripture stories of those who benefitted and were blessed, the following happened to me in the work setting...

I was a government employee for many years and had reached the highest automated pay increase for my grade. There had been jobs I qualified for, but others were chosen. Once the newly-hired person came on board, I was often tasked with training them! Nonetheless, I kept doing my best. Then, after years of being passed over by several people, **MY BLESSING OF A GOOD PROMOTION CAME!** I was temporarily promoted two grades at once and held that job for a year—publicizing the military installation and improving their customer service. ***BUT WAIT!* GOD WAS NOT THROUGH WITH ME YET!**

After a year in that position, I was called back to my former job with an adjusted salary. Eventually, by continuing to submit applications, I was selected for a three-grade higher position at another installation in the state! **TO SAY I FELT BLESSED AND ELATED IS AN UNDERSTATEMENT!** Yes, patience, hard work, dedication, and treating others right again gave me the **REWARD! *PRAISE GOD!!!***

BIBLICAL STORIES OF PATIENCE, DELAYS, AND SUFFERINGS

"Wait on the LORD: be of good courage, and He shall strengthen thine heart: wait, I say, on the LORD."

(Psalm 27:14)

David was a shepherd boy sought out while he was young and anointed for greatness. His story spans several chapters, beginning in the Book of 1 Samuel, verse 16. He was anointed to replace King Saul over Israel. The story is long and involved, with King Saul finding out and making attempts to kill David. Eventually, King Saul was killed by others, and David became the next king. Even though he made some serious leadership mistakes, David was still forgiven and loved by God.

The most notable blessing is that King David is listed as an ancestor of Jesus Christ! Although an angel told Mary she would bear a child, the earthly father Joseph was a descendant of David. Once he married Mary, it was a legal adoption of the son Jesus Christ she would bear!

David exercised patience as he awaited becoming the King of Israel many years before the promised Messiah would be born. Then, in God's timing, Mary and Joseph were blessed to birth and care for the Savior, Jesus Christ.

You cannot hurry our God because His timing is always **PERFECT!**

Genesis 18 tells the story of Abraham and Sarah. Sarah could not bear a child for Abraham; however, in his old age (and Sarah's as well), a son Isaac was born. God knew the deep love the couple had for Isaac, but God tested their love when Abraham was told to take the child and offer him as a sacrifice! As the story proves again, God's ways are not ours, and God provided a ram caught in the bush that was sacrificed in Isaac's place. The patience of the couple wanting a child seemed impossible. God proved it was possible! He continues to amaze and care for His people who love and serve Him. Isaac continued the family line by fathering Esau and Jacob. Further history is found as Genesis is read.

Joseph's story is well-known in many children's bible stories. Because his father Jacob favored him, Joseph was given a beautiful coat of many colors. That caused the older brothers to be jealous, and, eventually, when they were out together, they plotted a way to get rid of Joseph. Instead of killing him, they put Joseph in a deep well, eventually selling him to Midianite merchants who took him to Egypt.

Joseph was a dreamer and could interpret the dreams of others. In time, Joseph's dreams were made known to Potiphar, an officer of Pharaoh. When no one could interpret the reigning Pharaoh's troubling dreams, Joseph was brought forward and interpreted them perfectly. Joseph was rewarded and became a high-ranking officer during a famine in Egypt. As a result, in

God's perfect timing and Joseph's patience, he became a high official in Pharaoh's court. Eventually, he was reunited with his family during a severe famine. When Joseph's brothers came seeking food, they didn't even recognize him. The story is more involved but know that it all worked out. Joseph's family was brought to Egypt to live, and they were treated well.

Hannah's story is about another barren woman. She was very faithful in serving God. Her husband was Elkanah. Due to her love and dedication to God, she was eventually blessed with a son whom she named Samuel. Samuel means "heart of God." Hannah kept a promise she made to God when she became pregnant. After Samuel was weaned, she took him to Shiloh for dedication and religious training. The entire story is found in 1st and 2nd Samuel.

As a result of Hannah's patience and faithfulness, she was blessed. In the culture at the time, having male children determined a woman's worth, so she was dejected and considered a failure. To make things worse, Elkanah's other wife, Peninnah, was fertile. However, Hannah kept worshipping and praying to God. She did not give up! She prayed in her heart with her lips moving, but no voice was heard (1 Samuel 1:13). The Prophet Eli didn't understand what Hannah was doing; however, when she explained, he gave her his blessing, and she left in peace with her worries behind her.

Hannah's **PATIENCE** and diligence were noticed and blessed. She went her way, ate, and was no longer downcast (1 Samuel 1:18b). The depth of her prayers included promising to give her son to the Lord all the days of his life, and no razor would ever be used on his head (1 Samuel 1:11). That was in keeping with a Nazarite vow. Hannah's son Samuel was an honest, fair judge, and, as a prophet, he encouraged Israel to turn from idolatry and serve God only.

CONCLUSION

"And we know that all things work together for good to them that love God, to them who are the called according to His purpose..." (Romans 8:28)

Personal experiences and time have proven repeatedly that being patient is not an easy quality for me and most people I know. With the 78 years I have been blessed with, I have learned so many valuable lessons and am still working on each element of the Fruit of the Spirit. I sincerely pray my story helps someone along life's journey and is blessed!

In closing, I am sharing a few words from another poem that came to mind while drafting this Patience Fruit story:

"Remember the Fruit of the Spirit's blessings.
Apply each word to expand your spiritual worth;
Serving our God to the fullest extent possible
Will comfort you and countless others here on earth."

~~~~~~~~~~

"With all loneliness and meekness, with longsuffering, forbearing (patience) one another in love; and be renewed in the spirit of your mind; and that ye put on the new man, which God is created in righteousness and true holiness."
(Ephesians 4:22-24)

Patience: A Poem

By Marlowe R. Scott
© 2022

Patience is needed along life's way;

An attribute to develop

Throughout each living day.

Indeed, without it,

Events will go off course.

Never forget to seek it

Constantly, while traveling toward

Eternity's open doors!

"IMPATIENCE... Consider the cost."

Marlowe R. Scott

~~~~~~~~~~

"Lost PATIENCE... Wasted time."

Marlowe R. Scott

The Pressure of "The Wait"
By Angela R. Edwards

*"You are the people of God; He loved you and chose you for His own. So then, you must clothe yourselves with compassion, kindness, humility, gentleness, and **patience**."* (Colossians 3:12, Good News Translation (GNT) (emphasis added))

Admittedly, writing my "Patience" story did not come easily, but it's not for the reasons one might think. It's not because I did not want to be authentic. It's not because I wanted to "hide" behind my truth. No. It's simply because I am very patient (which often translates to being tolerant of a lot of mess). That, my friend, is the place where one of my strongest traits (patience/tolerance) actually proves to be a weakness.

Let me explain.

A couple of years ago (from the date of this writing), I penned my domestic abuse survivor story in its totality in a book titled *The Bathroom Was My Dungeon: True Tales of Surviving an Abusive Marriage*. You might be surprised to learn it took me 25 years to finally feel "safe enough" to share. That time in my life was tumultuous. The 25 years that followed were guilt- and shame-laden. Believe it when I say I **never** thought abuse would be a part of my life's story, but it was. I will not recount all the instances of abuse here; just know that my tolerance-turned-patience in that relationship led me into the deepest bowels of what became my "Hell on Earth."

To help you better understand my story moving forward, I will share a little about who I now call "The Former Me." In a nutshell, I was (and, by nature, still am) a nurturer. I blindly believed my love for any given person could effect change in their life. I'm sure someone reading this can relate to that delusion. While we are commanded throughout the Holy Bible to love, with one prominent instance found in Leviticus 19:18 to love our neighbor as we do ourselves, that alone cannot bring about change. As for me, it took my very spirit being broken by my former husband to realize one critical factor regarding my patience: No matter how much I tolerated his antics and abuse—believing I could love him free and clean—he was not going to change "just for me." What a painful lesson that was.

Moving along…

More recently, I listened to a sermon preached by Rev. Dr. Charles E. Goodman, Jr. from Tabernacle Baptist Church (Augusta, Georgia). As part of his "Rebuild" series, he spoke about Nehemiah's patience as he awaited approval from the king to leave the confines of Babylon and go to Jerusalem to rebuild the wall. Scripture tells us that he waited over four months to hear from the king one way or another. **FOUR MONTHS!** Can you imagine how extenuating that wait was for Nehemiah? I envision him becoming anxious every time he saw the courier in the area, only to be disappointed when it wasn't his time to receive a response from the king. Four months is a long time to wait for an answer to what seemed like a simple "yes" or "no" question, but Nehemiah waited patiently…and prayerfully.

Rev. Goodman's sermon truly spoke to me. I found myself reflecting on my former marriage and how I often patiently prayed for my now-ex-husband to get his life together.

I must pause here and state that he and I were unequally yoked, so our marriage was likely destined to fail from the start—but I was in love and didn't see the forest for the trees. As I reflected on those painful days of my life, I thought about my patience regarding dealing with my ex. The mental abuse was constant, yet I found a way to keep smiling...all while believing things would get better one day. I tolerated so much *unnecessarily*, including being physically abused. Today, I am stronger than ever for the choice I made to leave and divorce him.

Again, tough lesson but a lesson learned.

Throughout our lives, patience looks different for each of us. Whether we're waiting a few hours, one day, four months, or ten years, how we operate under the pressure of "THE WAIT" helps to determine our individual levels of patience. While someone may have the patience of Job, another may snap in the blink of an eye. It is something that cannot be taught. Either we have the gift, or we don't.

Now, don't get me wrong: There is no right or wrong way to practice patience. I believe some things call for an immediate response, such as keeping a child out of harm's way. For example, you wouldn't sit back and watch a child innocently reach for a boiling pot of water and say, "I'll wait until they touch the handle to react." No. If you see it happening, patience is not something you would put into practice. Conversely, if your loved one is plucking at your last nerve over something they've done repeatedly, you can choose to react quickly (and often negatively) or simply remove yourself from the situation.

Choices. As adults, we all have them.

In choosing to be 100% transparent here, while I can honestly say I have a high level of patience, I have absolutely none when it comes to tomfoolery. I recall a time when my children were little, and my home was "the place to be" for their friends and our neighbor's children. Far too often, the neighbor's children would come to our house when they got out of school because their mother wasn't home. I **never** minded watching them because I knew they were *safe*. Then, the day came when I was unable to make it home on time after a doctor's appointment, no matter how I rushed to make it. At the time, I didn't have a backup plan in place for my children because they could count on me to always be home when they arrived.

Well...

On that particular day, I arrived home roughly 15 minutes after they got off the bus. I parked in the driveway, frantic because I didn't see them anywhere around. As a matter of fact, none of the neighborhood children could be found. I ran down the street to one of my neighbors and asked if my children were there. She said, "No, I haven't seen them." Talk about freaking **OUT**! I then went to my neighbor's house directly across the street and asked the same thing. She actually lied and responded she hadn't seen them either. I was in a full-blown panic at that point.

WHERE WERE MY BABIES?!

As I walked back across the street in near tears, my daughter peeked her head around the corner from behind the house. Shortly after, my son did the same. I ran to them, embraced them, and asked, "Why are you back here???" The response floored me.

My daughter replied, "She (pointing to the neighbor's house across the street) told us to sit back here until you came home."

Wait. What? The same woman whose children I watched nearly daily in her absence told my children to do what?! I was livid! My mama bear kicked into overdrive that day. In response, I said and did things to that woman I am not ashamed to say I did—and would do again in a heartbeat, should the need arise.

Why did I choose to share that specific story, you might ask? Because from that day forward, I no longer practiced patience with my neighbor's "Missing-in-Action" moments. I do believe my point was made the day she basically abandoned my children, caring nothing for their welfare. No longer did I have to find myself obligated to watch her children because she ensured someone was home to receive them **EVERY** day after that.

Just think: Had I practiced patience/tolerance that day, nothing would have changed in her life or the lives of her children.

SIDENOTE: I knew enough not to involve the children in our spat, so they remained constant friends amid our grown-up mess.

Losing my head over a situation happens seldomly. For the most part, I am a level-headed person, able to respond to issues that arise with relative calm. When I am tested, however, I can and will rise to the occasion. I don't like having to do that, though. It feels like I'm being pulled out of character.

I want you to take a moment to consider what patience looks like in your own life. Are there areas where you recognize it as both a strength and weakness? Does one aspect shine brighter than the other? How can you make a change to build your level of patience with others...and yourself?

Here's the thing: Some people never truly "get it." Perhaps it's not theirs to get. I, however, implore you to seek out the root of any issues you may have with patience and address them head-on. Don't allow the enemy to keep that stronghold—that lack of patience—over you for one second longer. Ask God to strengthen you in **whatever** area(s) you may be weak and believe He will do it because you asked in faith.

In closing, **PATIENCE** is the Fruit of the Spirit that enables us to persevere under pressure. When we are faced with wrongdoings or being mistreated, it is ***this*** Fruit that maintains the qualities of love, joy, and peace. In response, when we are forced in the other direction, having patience means we will not retaliate but rather address those underlying motivations. With *God's Patience Fruit,* choose to look to Jesus for strength and the ability to refrain in situations that would otherwise deplete our resolve.

> "When we put our problems in God's hands, He grants us the patience to endure."
>
> Angela R. Edwards

Patience: A Universal Lesson
By Laurie Benoit

Throughout my life, I have learned that patience is something some people develop more naturally than others. Then, there are those (like me) who must learn to mature and grow into it.

We all have moments that teach us patience. As for me, there have been many lessons on patience in my life, but two truly exceptional ones stand out—both being deep, personal loves: parenthood and photography.

Photography is not only a hobby of mine but also a passion. It is one of the things that has taught me a great deal about patience but in a completely unique and new perspective from parenthood. Photography is the act of continually waiting for that "perfect moment in time" in which to capture its essence. It takes patience to capture the exact moment of exquisite color illuminating from a sunrise. Patience is seeking the perfect spot. Patience is waiting for each of the different seasons to arrive. See? It is all about having patience!

One of my favorite nature quotes is:

"Nature does not hurry, yet everything is accomplished." ~ Lao Tzu

Upon careful reflection of that quote, I have come to understand its simple truth: In nature, everything is accomplished in its own perfect time. Babies born in wildlife come in seasons. Flowers seemingly just know when it is time to bloom. The grass greens all on its own in the spring, and the trees' leaves fall when it is suitable for them. Everything happens in its own divine timing. It absolutely amazes me just how much nature has to offer in the way of lessons that we—as humans—could learn from if we only took the time and paid closer attention. Although this lesson on patience came quite a bit later in my life, its relevance is still very much welcomed going forward.

My photography is based on nature's landscape, and I have concluded that everything happens only in divine timing. There is no rushing nature in my moments behind the lens of a camera, for if I forged ahead of time, I would miss opportunities (as I have learned time and again).

Because I have witnessed an entirely different perspective of patience through my photography, I now embrace what one might consider a *"regular moment"* in time. What really happens around me fully engulfs my presence in the moment. Everything is new and distinctive, from the little giggle from a child and their natural curiosity to learn about everything around them to how the wind blows and livens the chimes just outside the window where I spend my time writing.

But there was a time when none of that would have captured my attention as it does now.

The fact is that I am a survivor of generational trauma and abuse. For most of my life, I had the patience of a stampede of wild horses. Usually, my feelings and the actions that followed would resemble that of an ocean storm, unstable and volatile at best. Patience was simply not a word in my vocabulary—until one day...

As I grew into adulthood, the day came when I became pregnant, and patience would become a new lesson—a new test. Nine long months of patience were ahead of me, waiting for my child to be born. Then, as time progressed, a new form of patience developed: motherhood. I had to practice patience as I allowed my child to grow, develop, and learn as only a child can with their curious nature. I had to practice patience not just with them but with myself, too. After all, parenthood is the ultimate lifelong job of learning and practicing patience! (If you're a parent, I'm sure you recognize that no two children are ever the same.) For me, parenting was completely new territory because it was a job that required me to be an untaught, patient person. Why would I classify myself as such? I never had anyone to teach, mentor, or guide me as I worked through those moments in which I desperately required patience.

So, needless to say, I have definitely had some downfalls in the parenthood lesson. In fact, it has been one of the most challenging lessons I've ever endured due to the lack of patience received in my own life.

To give a little backstory...

As a child, I was forced—at a very young age—to grow up and protect myself at all costs. Today, I recognize that is why I probably largely have had difficulty being patient with others in my life. Because of that, my children and I have suffered. To be honest, I found it extremely difficult to be patient with my children when so many outside factors contributed to my lack of patience for much of my life. When I became a mother, the abuse I had previously endured (which was still unhealed), coupled with more abusive relationships, kept me from becoming the mother that was required of me.

I acknowledge that is wholly on me.

With my two eldest children already living with their father, that right there was a pretty good indicator of how little I trusted myself and my own level of patience. The plain truth is this: It had taken me until my very last pregnancy (with three children already born to me) to really understand the depth of patience required when it came to parenting.

My last child, however, was my ultimate test in patience.

Now, I knew (and now know) there are people who have endured much more than I as it relates to enduring issues with their child(ren), but for me, I was truly put to the supreme test. When adding a medical issue (colic) to everything else I already had on my plate, I am surprised I wasn't an absolute recipe for disaster!

By definition, **colic** is a condition that can cause severe, often fluctuating pain in the abdomen caused by intestinal gas or obstruction in the intestines and suffered especially by babies.

My fourth and final child was colicky for nine long months, and with no real support from **anyone**—including her own father, who resided with me—I did everything I could possibly think of to comfort my daughter, yet it seemed nothing eased her pain. I slept very minimal hours with her in my arms and on my chest **every** night. Two solid hours of sleep was a "good night." Anything less was normal, and anything more was exceptional. However, throughout the day, it was the same routine of continuous, nonstop crying and pain. It felt as though I was forever holding my baby in my arms because nothing but the comfort of me holding her seemed to relieve her distress. And honestly, I'm not even certain motherly love was of any real comfort to her.

With the small amounts of sleep I had, there were times when I couldn't help but break down in tears out of frustration, feeling tremendously helpless and so alone. ***Was there anyone in my life willing to help me with this child?!*** Anyone who offered assistance would return her to me in literally a matter of minutes. Bathroom breaks were a welcome relief, if only for a moment.

Patience had become the only thing that helped me keep my sanity. The recognition that this little being required me to be as patient as I could possibly be with her as I worked through those very demanding and exhausting moments kept me "level" at best. To say the very least, it was the most significant lesson in patience I had ever learned in parenthood and in life. And even though I somehow mustered strength during that period in time, it was actually not long after that when my life spiraled out of control in a downward trend.

See, my relationship was very emotionally and mentally abusive and unstable. I had been isolated from everyone I knew, in a city I began to despise, with a person I grew to hate. I hated myself for feeling that way, too. Why? Because I never believed in using the word "hate" just because of the negative strength it implies. The time came when I decided to leave—to get out of that place, even if that meant leaving my partner. I didn't care anymore. I just wanted out.

But before that happened and after months of living in that hated city, I received a phone call from public health. They called to see when I would get the childhood inoculations done for my kids. I explained I had no healthcare and couldn't get them done. In response, I was told they didn't care if I had healthcare; they wanted my kids to be protected from possible childhood diseases, regardless. That appointment changed the coming months and the timing when I would finally see some reprieve.

I took my children to get their shots, and while at the hospital, the nurse decided to go the extra mile by checking them over carefully and taking their height, weight, etc. She then asked if I had any other concerns. Without my mentioning it, the nurse asked, "How long has your daughter been colicky?" I explained it had almost been since birth and that my previous doctor had told me she required the formula she was on. When she asked for the formula's name, she immediately stated, "Get her off that formula!" She then explained that it was one commonly known for causing colic.

I inhaled and exhaled deeply as I thought about what the nurse had just said. *After all those months, all I needed to do was change her **formula**?!* Then, it hit me all at once. I was angry at my previous doctor. I was relieved that the "cure" was something so simple. I was looking forward to sleeping peacefully. I was worried about how I would afford a more expensive formula. Ultimately, I was hopeful the colic would end with that one change.

It did! It took about three months or so for her body to adjust to the new formula, but she adjusted well. Once she got adjusted to the new formula, I decided it was time to move back to the city where I previously resided. Shortly after, it was time to make yet another change to my daughter's diet and get her on actual food. However, because of the colic, I was instructed to make the transition slowly and keep her on the formula a bit longer. Ultimately, it paid off.

That time, it was not just about patience. Upon my return to the city where my youngest had been born, I learned many more lessons. Those rounds of lessons took me on that downward spiral trend I mentioned earlier. It continued until I hit rock bottom and had to claw my way out of the mess I had made of my life and that of my children.

In the end, however, I emerged with the strength I needed to continually move forward, upward, and into a healthier brand of living for myself and those little beings who entirely relied on me to become a better person.

If there is one thing I have learned from parenthood, it is this: Being a parent is one of the most demanding jobs on earth, and there will always be times when patience is required as you are tested to the very brink.

May we always be reminded that children also learn from us what they see. They are like little sponges, soaking up absolutely everything we do. May we always be reminded to treat our little beings with the love and patience we wish to see in the world.

> *"Through patience, we learn the lessons of divine timing & growth in all its imperfections."*
>
> — Laurie Benoit

~~~~~~~~~~

> *"Patience encourages growth and maturity."*
>
> — Laurie Benoit

God Has Me on Hold
By Tosha Dearbone

Lately, I have been examining my life and how God has been taking me on this journey, ensuring I recognize His presence in every area of my life. Has it been easy? Absolutely not. It often feels downright awkward, leaving me to feel as though God has a hold on me. I imagine you're probably wondering what exactly I mean when I say, "God has a hold on me." Come and take a walk with me while I share why I feel that way.

Growing up, it wasn't always peaches and cream. I come from a background of generational patterns of abuse. From the time I was in the womb, I was set up to encounter dark seasons—ones that hung around for far too long.

Being a young girl without an established identity was detrimental to my growth. I began looking for love in all the wrong places around the age of fifteen. I believed things were good until the cheating started, the lying intensified, and the "rough playing" began to occur. At the time, I didn't look at it as abusive because I never thought to classify those narcissistic behaviors as such. Manipulation was my boyfriend's biggest tactic when he played on my need to be accepted or loved by someone. You see, I didn't hear the words "I love you" often in my youth, nor was I made to feel as though my family wanted me around. As a result, my boyfriend would do just enough to make me stay around without me actually paying attention to all of the things he did. Not to mention I got pregnant at 15 and then again at sixteen. (I know that will sound a bit "off" for some, but unfortunately, I didn't keep the first one. I delivered a baby girl in 2016.) The day finally came when I said, "Enough is **ENOUGH!**" I left him alone—which wasn't that difficult, considering he had already moved on with his new girlfriend.

In 1999, I started attending a new school. You know how everyone tries to get with you when you're the "new girl"? I was HER. As I walked into the school, it felt like everyone's eyes were on me...staring. It turns out they were! LOL! After all, I am a beautiful female! However, there was one guy I locked eyes with. We exchanged numbers and began a relationship shortly thereafter.

Well, things were going quite well at first. Soon enough, I learned he was no different than my last boyfriend. As a matter of fact, he was considerably worse! Early on, he began play-fighting with me, cheating on me (of course), bringing women into my home when I wasn't there, and riding them around in my car. Oh. And let's not forget to add that his family even came to stay with me and used me. Yes, you read that correctly. When they were there, they would steal my car while I was asleep, and my jewelry "came up missing." On top of it all, I was the only one paying the bills!

SIDEBAR: When people have no respect for you, they will take from you and abuse you any way they see fit—especially when you have no real idea who you are.

Many nights, I cried to God, "Why me? What is wrong with me? Why does his family (and he) feel it's okay to treat me this way?" You would not be surprised to learn none of them had any remorse for their mistreatment of me.

I recall the night my boyfriend pulled up to the house with a woman in my car. At the time, I was pregnant and resting on the couch. I had no idea a woman was riding in my car until I got up and looked out the window. I then began yelling and talking crazy to him, telling him **OFF**. He acted as if he did nothing wrong! While I was screaming all up in his face, he pulled out a gun, put it to my head, and said, "Girl, I will **KILL** you!" I know it had to be the Lord speaking through my reply because I immediately said, "You are just going to have to kill me!" By then, I was SO done with his bad behavior and mistreatment. You will never guess his response...

He laughed in my face and said aloud, "This girl is crazy!" He then grabbed his belongings and left in another car with his brother and mystery woman.

Without thinking about my safety or my children, I jumped into my car and followed them. I unsuccessfully tried to hit them when they stopped at a stop sign. I know I could have gotten hurt or even in trouble for my actions, BUT GOD!

Well, God did it again. He removed me from another horrible situation that had gone on for far too long. It was almost as if God were trying to see if I was paying attention to my own patterns—ones that had me repeating what I had already been through. I believe He was trying to get my attention to let me know I am much more valuable than I was giving myself credit for. I needed to learn that I need not continue to play on my need to be wanted or loved to have the right people find value in me.

After that tumultuous relationship, I took a break from dating and having sexual relations with anyone for about five years. I invested my time in working on myself, which included getting more involved in church, trying to understand who I truly am, and focusing on being a better mom. After all, I endangered not only myself but my children as well. Those years went by quickly. I soon found myself getting back out there and indulging in some adult fun, including spending time in the clubs.

One particular night, I went to a club in south Houston called LaShawns. I was minding my own business when a man approached me. We vibed instantly. Now, remember: I hadn't been on the dating scene or been involved with anyone for a while. Immediately, his attention made me yearn for that unhealed part of me. Admittedly, I loved the attention. As the club was closing, he asked if he could come with me. Without hesitation, I said yes. Crazy... I know. He came over that night, and, of course, we slept together. (I knew nothing at all about him). I thank God that it wasn't a one-night stand. He continued to come around and even spent time with my children. Eventually, I met his family, and we got along well, too. Months passed by, and our relationship continued to grow. Things were going well, and then I found out I was pregnant. Being pregnant wasn't a bad thing; it was the nonsense that came after it.

After picking him up from his mother's house one night, I noticed a car following us as we got onto the beltway. The car was filled with females, and they were trying to run us off the road. Little did I know, one of the occupants was someone he was messing with. I had to think fast because I didn't want them to follow me home, and I knew I couldn't fight anyone because I was eight months pregnant. I quickly called my cousin, who told me not to go home and to lead them to her house. Sure enough, they followed all the way there. When I pulled up (with the carload of females right behind me), my cousin and her friends came running outside with bats and only God knows what else, swinging and cursing at them. Those women ran so fast, trying to get out of there! Some got back in the car, and others ran until they could catch a ride on the Metro bus.

All I could think about was why I continued to get myself into situations where the guy cheated and felt it was okay to treat me any kind of way. You might be wondering if I left him after that incident. Nope. I stayed in the relationship because I didn't want to be left raising another baby on my own.

For a while, things returned to normal. Then, one day, we went to take pictures, and his "sister" came with us. Boy, when I tell you, **ALL** hell broke out when we got back home! The two of them got into an argument about something, and I heard her say, "So, you're just going to continue letting her think I am your sister?" Talk about pissed! That man literally had an entire family living in my home day and night. They were around me constantly, just for me to inadvertently learn she wasn't even his "sister" at all! She was actually a woman he'd been sleeping with the entire time! My rage level was at ten! I wanted to go upside his head—with a cast iron skillet!

Instead, I dropped to my knees and asked God, "Why? Why me?! Am I such a horrible person that I can't even see when someone is not good for me? How could he do what he just did to me?"

Not long after that "revelation," I gave birth to our son. Not only did my boyfriend say the child wasn't his, but he also walked out of his son's life and mine. You read that right. He made a mess of my life yet somehow found a way to make me feel as though I was the one who failed in the relationship.

As life would have it, time went by, and I tried moving on with my life, which included starting a new job. I was a single mother of three and needed to turn some things around. After graduating from medical assistant school, I took a job at Thomas Care Center, working with adolescents with behavioral issues. Things were going well, and, of course, the men were always the ones who made me feel accepted. I soon began chatting it up and even accepted a date to the movies with the man who became my fourth "baby daddy." I know…I know: When was I going to learn? Every guy I met didn't have to be my next bed buddy.

Well, not even one month later, I was pregnant—but he was different. He made sure I was taken care of, my children wanted for nothing, and my bills were paid. That's right: He came into my life doing all the right things. I felt like I had finally won! HAHA! The devil gets the laugh yet again! Yep, you guessed it: He was cheating with his first "baby mama." How did I know? She had me listen in on a call when he was supposed to be heading to work but was on the phone, letting her know he was on his way to her house. All I can remember is crying extremely hard because I was going to be left with not just one child but four—and I was still getting into relationships that continuously made me feel unworthy.

When he returned home to me later that night, we began arguing. Quick pause: I forgot to mention he had put his hands on me once before.

That night, during our argument, I refused to allow him near me without some form of protection. I ran into the kitchen and grabbed a butcher knife. As he angrily approached me, I swung—not knowing I would actually cut him. I panicked and called the police without giving thought to the fact that I could be charged for the offense. When they arrived, the officer I spoke to asked if I wanted to press charges. I replied, "No, I just want him to leave."

Meanwhile, the other officer tried to convince my boyfriend to press charges against me because "it could have been worse than what it was," but he declined to proceed and said no. (THANK GOD!)

After that night, we mutually decided to go our separate ways. Even though all that drama occurred, to this day, he still makes sure his daughter is taken care of.

I found myself living the single life again and made a conscious choice to get my life back in order. I was even getting more in tune with the Word of God and what it truly meant for my life.

A few more years passed, and I started dating again. At one point, I even got engaged, but my discernment had grown stronger, and I saw the wickedness coming from a mile away before it got too far out of hand.

Enter 2022.

God began to allow me to see why He has me on hold. It is to ensure that I was healing and understood my worth so that when the time does come for the mate designed just for me, I will know he is the one sent by God. I've been single for almost eight years at the time of this writing. I am happy to say I am more aware of what I deserve. You know what? Waiting isn't so bad because I know the wait will be worth it. The bonus of my PATIENCE story is that I have learned more about who I am and know the love of God is sufficient.

"To endure patience is to accept whom you are becoming."

Tosha R. Dearbone

"Maturity comes along with patience as you grow."

Tosha R. Dearbone

Fighting My Way to Patience
By Desirae Jefferson

As I reflect on my life, I think about those times when I had little to no **PATIENCE**. As far back as I can recall, I was not one to wait on anyone or anything. I was always impatient…always doing "this or that"…never slowing down… constantly fighting…and seemingly always raising disrespectful children. I remember having to fight my way out of childhood. As a matter of fact, I went straight from being a young girl to a young girl with a baby. My "growing up" happened instantly— to the point that it has taken years for me to catch up with the early onset of adulthood and learn how to wait and be patient while waiting.

I used to sit alone, look out the window, and wonder, "Where is everyone? Where are the people who said they love me?" Those questions were often asked during the time when I was in a physically abusive relationship with my child's father. I believe he thought of himself as more of a man when he would beat me in front of other people. While I'm sure that made him feel good, it made me feel horrible. My self-esteem suffered greatly because of the abuse.

People told me I was a pretty girl. In my mind, I would reply, "A pretty dumb girl!" Why? Because in my naïve, young mind, I believed only a dummy would stay with an abuser. I even went so far as to call myself dumb when I looked in the mirror. My exact words were, "You are dumb as shit. Just look at you. You have nothing. You have no one." Years and years of abuse eventually took its toll on me, leaving me damaged, discouraged, and demoralized.

After the birth of our son, my son's father became even more abusive. I remember the time he threw a jar at my head, busting me wide open. I had to be rushed to the hospital that day to get over 20 staples to close the wound. To this day, I can still feel the scar. Imagine how hopeless I felt, especially knowing I had to make a decision that would alter my life and the lives of my children. If I wanted to live, practicing patience with that man could no longer be a factor—and I wanted to **LIVE**!

As my recovery progressed, I returned to work. Although I felt better physically, I kept quiet around "him" and made my evacuation plan in silence. I knew I needed to get my children and myself out of that horrible situation, but I had no one in my corner who I believed understood my plight. When I finally had enough of his abusive behaviors, I packed up and moved to a childhood friend's house with my children. I am grateful for my friend. She was so gracious to my little family and me, and her family received us with open arms. Amid my depression and shame, it was she who gave me hope, safety, and love.

During that time in my life, I spent a lot of time in a room all alone, hoping to figure out my next step. My friend knew I was looking for a place of my own, so she helped me first find a stable job. I recall the countless times she would tell me how amazing and pretty I was, but I wasn't interested in accepting her compliments at the time. I still felt horrible because my self-worth had been obliterated. I couldn't believe I allowed a man to take all I had. My soul was gone. My heart was numb. I didn't feel loved. To be honest, I still struggle with feeling loved to this day.

Moving forward...

In response to not being healed mentally from the abuse, my heart grew cold and cruel, and I distanced myself from everyone. Yes, I worked...but I felt penniless. Yes, I had clothes on my back...but they weren't "nice" clothes. Yes, my hair was kept neat...but I couldn't afford to go to the salon. It seemed as if I had nothing going for me at all. I had no real interests or hobbies, so I found myself surviving just enough to feed my children.

Suddenly, we were homeless. We went to live in a homeless shelter for a while—one that was so far away from what was familiar that no one ever visited or even called. I was sure that if I had died, no one would have been none the wiser because no one ever thought enough of me to check on me. Eventually, we went to live in a family shelter. The three of us in one room was far better than where we had come from, but I still cried out to God, "Please, help me!"

In my youth, I remember asking God to remove me from this earth. Before I had children of my own, I often wished I'd never been born. Coupled with the abuse dished out to me by the man who professed to love me, abandonment issues plagued my world. I needed **HELP**!

As my children got older and we adjusted to our new lives, I started to feel better again. I learned to sit with myself, indulge in self-love, and practice patience. Amid those moments of self-reflection, I realized my children needed a strong mother—and I needed them. The days turned into months, and the months turned into a year. The year that followed was absolutely amazing! I started a new job, we did more things together as a family, my housing allowance came through, and I even started a group for battered women.

SIDEBAR: I cannot fail to mention that individual mental health counseling helped me tremendously, and I recommend it to anyone who is enduring or has endured abuse.

With my increased confidence came a new level of patience. I finally felt a little bit better about myself, found a beautiful apartment, and went to school to be a Paralegal. Today, I am a Certified Paralegal and Process Server who works with attorneys and constables throughout the city of Houston, Texas, and beyond. The change in my life began when I released the shame of being a ***VICTIM***. By the grace of God, I am a survivor. I may not be where I want to be, but I will never stop striving to be all God has called me to be—and I will do so...**PATIENTLY**.

"Patience is the calm acceptance that things can happen in a different order than the one you have in mind."

~ David G. Allen ~

Patience Set Me Free from the Past
By Reyna Harris Goynes

Much like many others—perhaps even you—I have endured many hardships and trials. Regardless of what I've been through, my **PATIENCE** joined my husband and me in holy matrimony...a relationship that began long ago in our middle school years.

When we were in 6th grade at the tender age of 12, we didn't know about "love," but we were crushing on each other. Unfortunately, at the age of 16, he was incarcerated—which put a hold on us actually starting a relationship. I cannot fail to mention that my mom told him she didn't like what he was doing or the lifestyle he was living, so she told him to leave me alone.

Well, as time progressed, I moved on with my life. I was in a relationship with my two oldest sons' father for five years. The first year-and-a-half or so was good, but the three years that followed included the most disrespectful and abusive situations I never thought possible. During the latter part of our relationship, he was physically hurt in an accident. I stayed by his side and continued to put up with his nonsense as long as I could. Right before my second son turned one year old, I walked away. To this day, we still communicate, but there will never be an "us" again.

Years later, I entered into another relationship with the man who fathered my third and fourth children. I just knew it would be better than what I had previously encountered.

Unfortunately, I was wrong. For almost 15 years, I was abused in virtually every way possible. Were it not for God whispering to me, ***"DON'T GIVE UP YET!"*** I don't know where I would be today. Each time God whispered to me, I believed that man would change. Again, I was wrong. In June 2014, I decided it was time to walk away and never look back—a decision I do not regret whatsoever.

Moving forward to the present day...

After an almost 10-year incarceration, my husband was released from prison. We patiently waited a year before getting married. A few weeks later, our daughter was born. Her birth changed my husband's life tremendously. Plus, just when I thought my life couldn't get any better, God whispered to me, ***"I TOLD YOU TO STAY PATIENT! I GOT YOU, NO MATTER WHAT!"*** When God spoke those words to me, I knew he meant every single one of them. Why? Because the man he brought into my life in 2014 wasn't the same "kid" I knew in middle school. Although I was head-over-heels in "love" with him then, my feelings grew and matured for him more than ever.

I know we are just living the beginning of our story, but it is one I pray will help others work past their hurt. When you love someone, you must trust them...love them...and have patience with them always. I'm a witness. My **PATIENCE** was razor-thin before my husband came back into my life. He is truly the love of my life—the man I waited for **PATIENTLY**.

"Love is PATIENT, but it's also KIND."

Reyna Harris-Goynes

"Keep your faith while being PATIENT."

Reyna Harris-Goynes

Keywana Wright-Jones

Waiting in Silence
By Evangelist Keywana Wright Jones

Were there times in your childhood when you desired dessert—such as a chocolate ice cream cone—before dinner? If so, you likely received the following reply from your parent: "Not until after you eat your dinner." Meanwhile, you found yourself waiting in silence, envisioning two scoops of ice cream resting atop a cone. Perhaps you can recall when you purchased your first home or vehicle. You contacted the seller or visited the car dealership, anticipating the purchase to be virtually instantaneous...or at least within a few days. However, the reality was that it might have taken longer than expected, leaving you to **wait...in silence**.

So, how does one "wait in silence"? The Bible encourages us this way:

"Be anxious for nothing, but in everything by prayer and thanksgiving, let your request be made known to God" (Philippians 4:6-7).

After making our requests known to God through prayer and thanksgiving, we must then wait for God to fulfill them. Believe in your heart that He will do it. Even when it may seem hard to wait, wait anyway. I promise you: Your outcome will be better than if you tried to fulfill "it" on your own. Sometimes, God will show you a glimpse of your future through a dream or prophetic word. You must wait for it to come to pass—often in silence, ***especially*** if you choose not to share it with anyone.

I am reminded of Mary and Joseph. God sent an angel to tell Joseph that Mary would have a child. Joseph and Mary had to steal away in silence to protect themselves and their unborn child from the King's decree. Mary had to wait in silence for the Holy Child to be born.

Let me ask you this: **Are you willing to keep your promise to yourself until it is the appointed time to share with others?**

Waiting in silence can have significant benefits, though. Let's look at the story of Hannah. She desired a child, but God had shut her womb. She then decided to get God's attention, so she entered the temple and started pouring out her heart to God…in silence. Her mouth moved, but no words escaped her lips. The priest watched her, believing she was drunk—but she wasn't. In her silence, she asked God to fulfill her heart's desire. Psalm 37:4 states, *"Delight thyself in the LORD, and He will give you the desires of your heart."* Well, God honored her request, and she became pregnant! When you delight yourself in God, He will give you the desires of your heart, too!

"I wait for the LORD; my soul does wait, and in His Word, I put my hope" (Psalm 130:5)

When you wait on the Lord and meditate on His Word, you can put your hope in Him. When you place your hope in Him, what you are waiting for will come to pass in your life. Be patient. Wait for it. Hannah had hope in the Lord. After years of disappointment and depression from being unable to conceive, she changed her mindset and began putting her hope in God. Year after year, she went to the temple with her husband, but when she found herself at a crossroads, Hannah realized she had to put **HER** hope in God.

Do **YOU** have that level of patience and hope in the Lord?

Rest assured that it is okay to wait in silence and put your trust in Him. Don't allow others to steal your hope. Don't let people make you think you move ahead of God's promise to bring your *"it"* to pass. Consider the story of Abraham and Sarah. They thought they could bring forth a child their way instead of believing what God told them: Sarah would become pregnant in her old age. Scripture tells us that Sarah told Abraham, "I have a plan. Go and sleep with your handmaid servant." That went against what God had **promised** them. He promised the couple a child of their own. All they had to do was wait patiently for it to come to pass. You can't force God's hand. When He makes a promise, it is His "job" to keep it. Get out of God's way and let Him do the impossible in your life!

Rest in the Lord and wait on Him (see Psalm 37:7). When you rest in Him, you release that *"it"* and put your trust in Him. You will soon come to know for yourself—without a shadow of a doubt—that God will do just what He said. You will be able to wait patiently for that new car, a new home, or a new job. You will be able to encourage yourself.

There were many times I had to wait patiently on the Lord and put all my trust in Him. Tolerating the delay wasn't always easy, but it happened just as it should have for me. Always remember: **Our timing is not God's timing.** Recall the story of Jesus' friend Lazarus who was dead for four days. Lazarus' sister came crying to Jesus, saying, "If you were here, Lazarus would not have died!" Four days later, Jesus raised Lazarus from the dead.

When you wait on God patiently, you come out as a winner **every** time. Trust and believe that whatever *"it"* is that God has for you will come to pass in your life.

Let us pray:

Heavenly Father, we ask that You help us to be patient with the promises You have for us. Help us to put our trust in Your Word and not doubt. When we ask, help us believe the supernatural will come to pass. Help us to get out of Your way so that You can have Your way in our lives. Amen.

"The two hardest tests on the spiritual road are the patience to wait for the right moment and the courage not to be disappointed with what we encounter."

~ Paulo Coelho ~

Conclusion

Thank you for taking this **PATIENCE** walk with us. We hope and pray that something you've read spoke to a situation that has kept you bound in regret, shame, and guilt. We hope and pray that as of today...right now...right this very moment, you are finally released from that "thing."

Always be mindful that circumstances will arise that will require immediate action without forethought. That's part of the human experience. As long as we are alive, we have choices to make. How we react to any given situation could be the difference between life and death—literally. Practice **PATIENCE** often.

You are further encouraged to reflect on your life and gain further clarity on your **PATIENCE** walk by engaging with the question-and-answer section that follows. Although geared toward those on their Christian journey, each question is intended to prompt deep contemplation on how your life can be changed for the better.

We will not always grasp the significance of our **PATIENCE** walk, especially after losing it with others. As soon as we reach that place of calmness, might we consider how the situation could have been handled differently? Should we pause to think about those who look up to us with great expectations of how we model our Christian walk and lives?

One of my *favorite* **PATIENCE** quotes comes from Brian Weiss:

"Inner peace is impossible without patience. Wisdom requires patience. Spiritual growth implies the mastery of patience. Patience allows the unfolding of destiny to proceed at its own unhurried pace."

So, my friend, I pray the stories contained herein changed your life and outlook in some way. Many people have shared with me how each Fruit of the Spirit book in the series to date have touched their souls and blessed them beyond measure. They see they're not alone and that they share similar stories with the contributors. That in itself reminds me of the God-inspired purpose for this series:

We are blessed to be a blessing to others!

~~~~~~~~~~

If you are interested in joining us on this ***God's Fruit*** journey by sharing your story in upcoming publications, please contact Angela Edwards at RedeemedByHim@RedemptionsStory.com for details and to be added to the contact list.

It's Time to Reflect on Your Patience Level

What situation(s) make it challenging for you to be patient?

_____
_____
_____
_____
_____
_____
_____
_____
_____
_____
_____
_____
_____
_____

God's Patience Fruit

What action(s) do you take to change your patience level during those difficult times?

God's Patience Fruit

When you hear "wait on the Lord," what does that mean to you?

God's Patience Fruit

Which "Patience Fruit" story has resonated the most with you and why?

God's Patience Fruit

*What is **YOUR** "Patience Fruit" story?*

God's Patience Fruit

God's Patience Fruit

About the Compiler

Angela R. Edwards is the CEO and Chief Editorial Director of Pearly Gates Publishing, LLC (PGP) and Redemption's Story Publishing, LLC (RSP) — Award-Winning International Christian Book Publishing Houses located in the Atlanta, Georgia area — and the Founder of the Battle-Scar Free™ Movement, a recognized 501(c)(3) nonprofit created to assist victims and survivors of domestic violence and abuse through one-on-one support and community outreach. In May 2018, PGP was honored as the 2018 Winner of Distinction for Publishing in South Houston, Texas, by the Better Business Bureau (BBB). In 2019 and in the years since, her companies have been awarded BBB Gold Star Certificates for their exemplary service to their clients and community.

Angela's mantra is ***"My Words Have POWER!"*** Since its inception in January 2015, PGP has been blessed with an ever-growing and diverse group of over 100 authors who have penned topics related to faith, love, abuse, bullying, Bible study tools, marriage, and so much more. Their youngest published author was only two years old; their eldest is 78 years old at the time of this publication. To their credit and God's glory, PGP and RSP have over 150 Bestselling titles collectively to date.

An affordable publishing option (in comparison to some of the large, traditional publishing houses), PGP and RSP work one-on-one with authors to ensure financial hardship is not a discouraging part of the publishing process. For those desiring to share their God-inspired messages for the masses, including both new and 'seasoned' authors, both publishing houses provide unique services and support that many have said "left them feeling as if they are the only author" placed under each company's care.

The Holy Bible states that *"God loves a cheerful giver"* (2 Corinthians 9:7). To that end, PGP and RSP frequently host fantastic giveaways and contests. Throughout the past few years, new author contests have awarded contestants over $15,000 in services total.

In addition to the aforementioned, Angela is a domestic abuse survivor. Since first telling her abuse-survivor story publicly, she has become a **"Trumpet for Change."** The Battle-Scar Free™ Movement is a product of her story. As part of her God-given mission, she provided abuse victims and survivors **FREE** opportunities to anonymously share their testimonies in a book series titled *God Says I am Battle-Scar Free*. Although the seven-book series is now complete, Angela's mission to help individuals heal with the power of their words continues. Assisting others with the healing process is paramount to her, which propelled her to become a volunteer Domestic Violence Liaison for the Star of Hope Mission in Houston, Texas. Furthermore, you are encouraged to connect with her 501c3 nonprofit domestic violence awareness organization at www.bsfmovement.org to learn more and become a supporter... a **Trumpet for Change**!

Angela holds an A.A. Degree in Business Administration from the University of Phoenix and is working towards her B.S. Degree in Psychology with a concentration in Christian Counseling from LeTourneau University. She is a woman of God, wife, mother, grandmother of 20, and trusted friend. Originally a New Jersey native, she has since made Georgia her home and embraced the southern culture to the fullest. She loves life and affirms daily:

"NOT TODAY, SATAN! UH-UH! NOT TODAY!!!"

> "You cannot force God's hand. Practice PATIENCE."
>
> Angela R. Edwards

Other Books in the Series

God's Love Fruit (2019)

God's Joy Fruit (2020)

God's Peace Fruit (2021)

Made in the USA
Middletown, DE
20 October 2022